HURRICANES, TSUNAMIS,
AND OTHER NATURAL DISASTERS

Previous page: St. Mark's Square in Venice, Italy, lies under five feet of water after a violent storm hit the city in 1996.

This page: A volcanologist collects samples of lava from Mount Etna in Sicily, Italy. In the background a fountain of lava erupts from the volcano, which is the most active in Europe.

HURRICANES, TSUNAMIS,
AND OTHER NATURAL DISASTERS

Andrew Langley

Foreword by
Bill McGuire

KINGFISHER

BOSTON

Editor: Clive Wilson
Coordinating editor: Caitlin Doyle
Senior designer: Peter Clayman
Picture research manager: Cee Weston-Baker
Senior production controller: Lindsey Scott
DTP coordinator: Catherine Hibbert
DTP operator: Claire Cessford
Artwork archivist: Wendy Allison
Proofreaders: Sheila Clewley, Terri McCargar
Indexer: Clive Wilson

KINGFISHER
a Houghton Mifflin Company imprint
222 Berkeley Street
Boston, Massachusetts 02116
www.houghtonmifflinbooks.com

First published in 2006
10 9 8 7 6 5 4 3 2

2SBF/0406/TWP/MA(MA)/130ENSOMA/F

LIBRARY OF CONGRESS CATALOGING-IN-PUBLICATION DATA
Langley, Andrew.
Hurricanes, tsunamis, and other natural disasters/by Andrew Langley.—1st ed.
    p. cm.—(Kingfisher knowledge)
Includes index.
1. Natural disasters—Juvenile literature. I. Title. II. Series.
GB5019.L364 2006
363.34—dc22   2005027200
ISBN 0-7534-5975-2
ISBN 978-07534-5975-1

Printed in Singapore

NOTE TO READERS
The web site addresses listed in this book are correct at the time of publishing. However, due to the ever-changing nature of the Internet, web site addresses and content can change. Web sites can contain links that are unsuitable for children. The publisher cannot be held responsible for changes in web site addresses or content or for information obtained through third-party web sites. We strongly advise that Internet searches are supervised by an adult.

GO FURTHER . . .
INFORMATION PANEL KEY:

web sites and
further reading

career paths

places to visit

Contents

▼ A violent earthquake in 1999, which killed more than 2,400 people, caused this building to collapse in Taipei, Taiwan.

Foreword

Our wonderful planet earth provides for all our needs. It gives us water to drink, fertile soils in which to plant our crops, wind to fly a kite, and snow to let us race down a mountainside on a snowboard. But it also has a dark side. The gentle rains can become a torrential downpour that feeds raging floodwaters, the fertile soils on the flanks of volcanoes can be buried beneath rivers of molten lava, while the whispering breezes and snow flurries can become devastating storms and freezing blizzards.

Studying natural hazards, such as storms, earthquakes, and volcanic eruptions, can be dangerous—but also very rewarding. On a dark September night almost ten years ago I was working as a volcanologist on the beautiful Caribbean island of Montserrat. I was woken up by a growing rumble that sounded exactly like a jumbo jet taking off. The noise wasn't an aircraft but Montserrat's Soufriere Hills volcano blasting into life. Within seconds a huge cloud of ash had surged into the sky, and small lumps of rock clattered onto roofs and cars. This was really scary. We didn't know how big the eruption was going to be, or even if we would survive, but we had to get to work. Almost one thousand people were still living in the volcano's immediate vicinity, and they needed help to leave the danger zone. With a couple of colleagues I drove toward the volcano to find out what was going on and to offer assistance to terrified men, women, and children. Fortunately, the eruption only lasted 45 minutes, and no one was killed or injured, but its memory will always be with me. If the explosion had been much larger, neither I nor my colleagues would be here to tell the tale. When the ash had cleared and the morning dawned bright and sunny, it felt good to be alive and to have helped evacuate so many people.

Natural hazards will always be with us, and people will always be needed to try to understand the processes that cause them, to monitor them and predict when they might happen next, and to try to prevent them from leading to great disasters such as the Indian Ocean tsunami or the recent devastation in New Orleans by Hurricane Katrina. This book is called *Natural Disasters*, and it provides a fantastic introduction to the science of natural hazards, their effects, and how we might cope with the worst they can throw at us. Hopefully, it will inspire you to learn more about these awe-inspiring but dangerous phenomena and join the ranks of our future volcanologists, earthquake scientists, or storm chasers. There will always be more that we need to know, and as the population of our planet increases and global warming begins to take hold, an increasing number of hazards and even bigger disasters mean that we will need all the help we can get. Good luck!

Professor Bill McGuire
Benfield Professor and Director, Benfield Hazard Research Centre, England

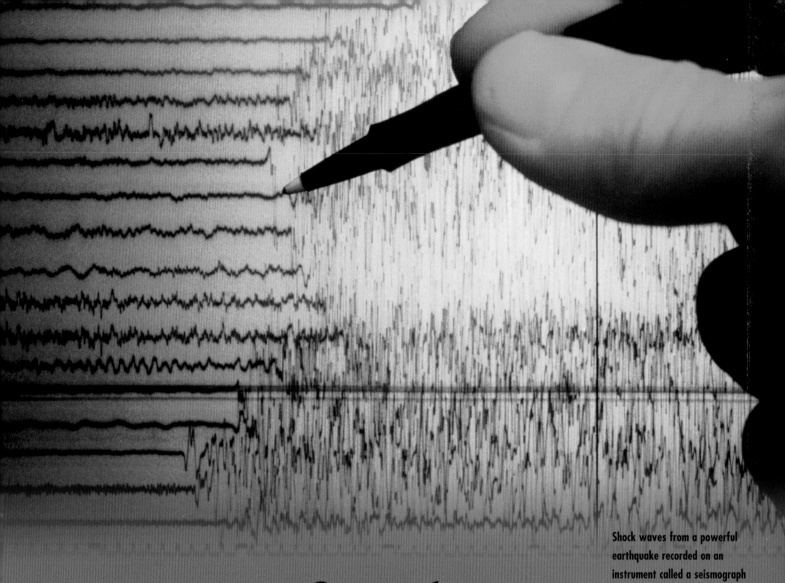

Shock waves from a powerful earthquake recorded on an instrument called a seismograph

CHAPTER 1

The restless earth

Every year there are around one million earthquakes throughout the world. Most are minor tremors that take place far below the ground. But occasionally a much more powerful earthquake strikes, unleashing the equivalent energy of several nuclear bombs. When major earthquakes happen close to densely populated areas, they can cause catastrophic damage. They shake and split the surface of the earth, destroying whole cities, killing thousands of people, and leaving many more people homeless. Earthquakes can also trigger massive waves called tsunamis. These build up into walls of water that flood low-lying coastlines, spreading the devastation over an even wider area. It has been estimated that during the last 100 years earthquakes have killed more than two million people across the planet.

▲ The shock waves from an earthquake cause buildings to collapse with devastating results. These cars were crushed like matchboxes during an earthquake at Northridge, near Los Angeles, California, in 1994. The quake killed 57 people.

Moving ground

The ground beneath our feet feels solid and still. But in fact, it is moving all the time. The outer layer of the earth is broken up into huge plates, like the pieces of a gigantic jigsaw puzzle. These plates are constantly in motion and are very slowly being pushed together or pulled apart. When they slide and clash against each other, the plates can produce shock waves, which we experience as earthquakes.

Floating world

Humans live on the surface of the earth's outer covering, which is called the lithosphere. This rocky layer, which can be up to 310 miles (500km) thick in places, includes the crust and the top part of the mantle. The lithosphere consists of seven major tectonic plates and several smaller ones. Below the lithosphere is the asthenosphere—a layer that is made up of molten and liquid materials. Scientists believe that the plates float on this layer, shifting by as much as two inches (5cm) in one year. This may not seem like very much, but it is enough to have far-reaching consequences, including earthquakes.

Seismic waves

Some plates move apart, allowing molten rock to well up through the gap from below and solidify. Others move together. This head-on clash of plates can have several results. The plates may pile up into mountain ranges over millions of years or grind alongside each other. The constant squeezing and stretching of the plate edges builds up stresses in the rock, which eventually rupture and cause an earthquake. The point directly above the earthquake is called the epicenter. The energy that is released travels outward in a series of seismic waves, or vibrations. These grow weaker as they travel farther from the epicenter, but they may still be felt as far as 992 miles (1,600km) away.

Rescue workers search for survivors in the ruins of a building after an earthquake in Taipei, Taiwan, in September 1999. The earthquake shook the whole island, destroying more than 10,000 homes and killing more than 2,000 people.

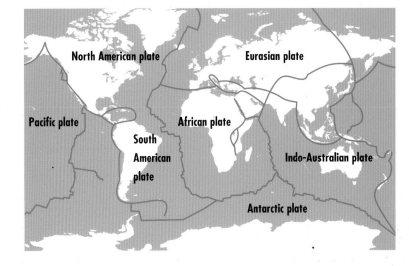

North American plate
Eurasian plate
Pacific plate
African plate
South American plate
Indo-Australian plate
Antarctic plate

▲ The surface of the earth is made up of seven main tectonic plates. Their movement is the cause of many of the planet's major processes such as the drifting of the continents, earthquakes, and volcanoes.

Danger zones

Almost all major earthquakes occur at the edges of the plates, where they meet. The world's main danger zone is at the border of the Pacific plate—a crack that runs around the rim of the Pacific Ocean. More than half of all earthquakes occur along this line, as well as many volcanic eruptions. The other big earthquake area is the belt that runs from the Mediterranean eastward to China, where the Eurasian plate meets the African and Indo-Australian plates.

Earthquake!

A great scar in the earth's crust runs for almost 600 miles (960km) along the coast of California. This is the San Andreas Fault, where the Pacific plate slowly grinds along the North American plate. On April 18, 1906, a sudden break in the rock shifted the ground by 20 feet (6m). This triggered an earthquake that rocked San Francisco and started fires that destroyed the downtown. More than 2,500 people were killed. In 1989 another major earthquake hit the area.

▲ The valleylike crack of the San Andreas Fault in California marks the boundary between two plates. During an earthquake the ground on both sides of the fault can move by up to 39 feet in a few seconds.

Earthquake-resistant buildings

Collapsing houses, fires, and floods cause most of the deaths that occur during earthquakes. Engineers have tried to develop ways of building houses that can survive seismic shocks in areas that are frequently hit by tremors. Light, two-story houses with timber frames suffer less damage than old-fashioned stone or brick houses. Some buildings are now constructed from very strong concrete with an outer wall of steel to make them less likely to collapse.

▼ The epicenter of the San Francisco earthquake in 1906 was very close to the city itself. Fires caused by broken gas pipes and arson burned a lot of the city down to the ground after the quake.

Vulnerable Japan

Japan lies at the meeting point of three tectonic plates—the Eurasian, the Pacific, and the Philippine. As a result, the country suffers from more earthquakes than any other part of the world. Almost ten percent of all seismic shocks happen in the region. In 1923 more than 150,000 people were killed by an earthquake. A more recent quake flattened the city of Kobe in 1995, killing 5,400 people.

South Asia earthquake 2005

Another danger area is the Himalayan mountains in south Asia, where one tectonic plate pushes into another. A major earthquake hit the Kashmir region on October 8, 2005. The tremors twisted the landscape and wrecked buildings over an area of 248 miles (400km) and shook parts of Afghanistan and India. Current estimates are that more than 70,000 died in the disaster.

▲ Almost 250,000 people were made homeless by the earthquake that hit Kobe, Japan, in January 1995. Despite near-freezing temperatures, many people chose to sleep outdoors in fear of aftershocks.

▼ In 1989 San Francisco suffered its most severe earthquake since the 1906 quake. More than 3,500 people were injured, and there were 66 deaths. At the time, it was the most expensive natural disaster in U.S. history.

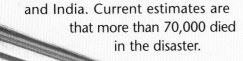

Tsunami terror

A stone that drops into a pond sends out a widening circle of ripples. In the same way, an earthquake under the sea creates a series of waves that can travel for many thousands of miles. These monster waves, called tsunamis, can have a terrible impact when they crash on land. Tsunami means "harbor wave" in Japanese. The term was originally used by fishermen who returned to their port to discover devastation in the surrounding area.

Earthquakes at sea

Most major tsunamis are caused by earthquakes on fault lines under or close to the ocean. A sudden upward or downward shift in the ocean floor acts like a giant paddle, pushing away an immense volume of the surrounding water. A series of waves—sometimes hundreds of miles apart—radiates out through the sea. In open water the crest of the wave is never very high above the surface. People in boats may not even notice that a tsunami has passed under them.

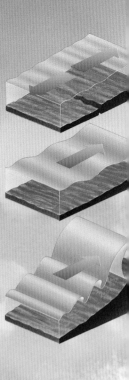

▶ Most tsunamis are the result of undersea earthquakes that cause the ocean floor to convulse. Underwater volcanoes and landslides can also trigger tsunamis.

▶ In open water a fast-moving tsunami wave may only reach three feet in height, but its immense energy extends down to the seabed.

▶ As it reaches the shore, the wave slows down and rapidly becomes steeper and taller. A series of tsunami waves may follow the leading one.

Fire raged through Lisbon for five days after it was struck by an earthquake and a series of tsunamis in 1755. Out of a population of 275,000, almost 90,000 people were killed.

Double disaster

Earthquakes and tsunamis are terrifying prospects on their own. But sometimes they strike together. On November 1, 1755, Lisbon, the capital of Portugal, suffered a major earthquake. Buildings fell, instantly burying hundreds of people. However, many people fled to the harbor, believing that they would be safe there. Soon afterward tsunamis raced in from the Atlantic Ocean, flooding the dock area and sweeping people to their deaths.

Hitting the coast

A tsunami can travel across the ocean at speeds of up to 500mph (800km/h), which is as fast as a jet aircraft. As it gets close to the coastline, the tsunami slows down, but it rapidly rears up to a great height. By the time it reaches the shore the wave can reach a height of 100 feet (30m) or more. The force of a tsunami can reduce buildings to rubble and can carry boats and boulders several miles inland.

▼ After traveling thousands of miles across the ocean, the destructive energy of a tsunami is released as it crashes ashore. The immense weight of water can destroy everything in its path.

▲ Animals often display unusual behavior before an earthquake or a tsunami. These Chinese government posters show people what to look out for before such an event.

The Indian Ocean tsunami

The tsunami on December 26, 2004, was one of the deadlie[r] natural disasters in recorded history. It began on the seabe[d] of the Indian Ocean, to the northwest of the island of Sumatr[a] Two tectonic plates meet at this point, and one slides undernea[th] the other. The huge stresses that build up at this fault line wer[e] suddenly released, triggering an extremely powerful earthquak[e]. As a result, the seabed was rapidly thrust upward by 66 feet (20m), displacing billions of tons of seawater.

▲ People flee in terror as the first tsunami crashes ashore on the Andaman Islands on December 26, 2004. The photographer who took this picture escaped unhurt, then watched two more giant waves from up on higher ground.

▼ Soldiers carry away a damaged fishing boat from a beach in southern India that was battered by the tsunami. In India alone more than 350,000 people were made homeless.

Panic on the beaches

Waves hurtled across the ocean in every direction. Within 30 minutes they had reached the coast of Sumatra to the east, crashing inland at a height of 66 feet (20m). The tsunami also raced farther north, toward the coast of Thailand. More waves, thousands of miles to the west, devastated the southern tip of Sri Lanka.

▲ Many countries (red) around the rim of the Indian Ocean were directly affected by the 2004 tsunami. The waves radiated from the epicenter, off the coast of Sumatra, Indonesia—even reaching the coast of east Africa.

Future recovery

More than 300,000 people died in the Indian Ocean tsunami, and many bodies were never recovered. Aside from the terrible loss of life, the disaster robbed the survivors of homes, possessions, food, clean water supplies, and vital farmland. A worldwide relief fund raised several hundred million dollars, but recovery will take many years.

Warning systems

When the tsunami struck, the Indian Ocean had no warning system, unlike in the Pacific Ocean. There a network of observatories monitors tide levels and indications of earthquakes. Information is sent to the Tsunami Warning Center in Honolulu, Hawaii, and people can be alerted far in advance of any impending tsunami.

▲ Many coastal communities were completely destroyed by the Indian Ocean tsunami. Six months after the disaster these Sri Lankan villagers were still clearing the rubble from their homes.

Understanding quakes

Ancient legends explained that earthquakes were the work of the gods. The Fijians of the Pacific believed that tremors were caused by the movements of the god who carried the world on his shoulders. An ancient Japanese myth told of a giant catfish that lived underground, creating earthquakes with its thrashing tail. Today scientists have a much greater understanding of seismic activity. Despite modern technology, however, earthquakes are still notoriously difficult to predict with any accuracy.

▲ A Chinese scientist designed this instrument around A.D. 32. Shock waves from an earthquake move a pendulum inside. This opens the jaws of the dragon that is facing the direction of the earthquake. A ball then falls into the mouth of the toad below.

▼ A seismologist at Taiwan's Central Weather Bureau in Taipei examines seismic waves produced by two earthquakes that struck Taiwan on June 14, 2001. Both measured more than six on the Richter scale, but, fortunately, there were no casualties.

Measuring equipment

One important instrument for earthquake detection is the seismograph, which can record underground movements. The first practical seismograph was developed by John Milne in 1880. A pen attached to a weight on a pendulum was supsended from a frame that was fixed firmly to the ground. Any seismic waves were recorded onto a roll of paper. Modern seismographs use electronic motion sensors, amplifiers, and recording equipment.

Waves

Earthquakes generate three different types of waves. A primary wave travels the fastest, and it can move through solid rock, as well as water and even molten magma in a volcano. It pushes and pulls the rock, causing vertical movement. A secondary wave distorts the rock, shearing it from side to side and making the ground move vertically and horizontally. A surface wave is like the ripple in a pond. It is produced by the first two types of waves when they are very close to the earth's surface.

The Richter scale

In 1935 Charles Richter devised a way of measuring an earthquake based on the energy that is released. A minor tremor ranks as two or less on the Richter scale. An earthquake that is more than five, however, is strong enough to cause structural damage to buildings. The most violent quakes generally measure eight or greater. The Indian Ocean tsunami in 2004 was triggered by a quake that was rated at 9.1—one of the most powerful that has ever been recorded. Another system—the Mercalli scale—is used to measure the effects on the surface such as chimneys falling down (VII), railroad track bending (X), and total destruction (XII).

Fire is a common hazard after an earthquake. These Japanese schoolchildren wearing fire-resistant head protection during an earthquake drill.

▶ Many modern seismographs use electronic sensors to detect tiny movements. Data is then transmitted to a computer. This device is monitoring seismic activity in Antarctica.

In case of emergency

If you are indoors when an earthquake occurs, you should stand next to a central wall in a building, or shelter under a strong table or stairway. Stay away from windows and outer doors. Do not move outdoors where there is a high risk of falling debris. If you are caught outside, it is best to stay out in the open and far away from chimneys, overhead power lines, and anything else that might collapse. After the tremors have finished it is still important not to get too close to damaged buildings because they are likely to be very unstable.

▲ In Parkfield, California, researchers have set up instruments, including laser systems, to monitor seismic activity that is caused by the San Andreas Fault.

SUMMARY OF CHAPTER 1: THE RESTLESS EARTH

Under the earth

The outer layer of the earth consists of huge, drifting slabs of rock called tectonic plates. These float on the mantle—a layer of molten and liquid rock that is deep underground. The plates are in constant motion, some drifting apart, some colliding, and others rubbing and squeezing against each other. The boundary between two plates is called a fault. Sometimes the plates "stick," and stress builds up in the rock at the edges of the plates. Eventually this ruptures and creates violent tremors—an earthquake. The energy from the rupture

moves outward in a series of vibrations called seismic waves. The point on the surface directly above the source of the seismic waves is called the epicenter. The waves grow weaker as they travel away from the epicenter. The

Extensive damage caused by an earthquake in Northridge, California

areas in the world that are at the most risk from earthquake are close to the fault lines. When an earthquake occurs on fault line under the sea, it can trigger a tsunami. A sudder upward or downward shift in the seabed shifts huge volume of water that form tsunamis. The waves can travel across the ocean at speeds of up to 500mph (800km/h). Out at sea th waves can pass unnoticed under a boat. When they reach the coast, however, they slow down and rear up in the shallow water. As it crashes ashore, a tsunami can reach up to 100 feet (30m) in height. The force of the impact can destroy everything in its path and cause severe flooding.

Measuring earthquakes

Although earthquakes are difficult to accurately predict, scientists constantly monitor earthquake activity worldwide They use instruments such as the seismograph for detecting movement under the ground. The size, or "magnitude," of an earthquake is measured on the Richter scale, based on the energy that is released by the quake, or the Mercal scale, which charts the damage that results.

Go further . . .

Track earthquakes throughout the world at: www.earthquakes.com

Find out more about earthquakes at: www.earthquake.usgs.gov

Learn more about the 2004 Indian Ocean tsunami at: www.pbs.org/wgbh/nova/tsunami/

Earthquakes in Human History by Jelle Zeilinga de Boer and Donald Theodore Sanders (Princeton, 2004)

Tsunamis by Luke Thompson (Children's Press, 2000)

Eyewitness: Volcanoes and Earthquakes by Susanna Van Rose (Dorling Kindersley, 2004)

Geomagnetist
Measures the earth's magnetic field and explores the planet's orgins.

Geophysicist
Studies the physics of the earth and the processes that take place inside our planet and on the surface.

Paleomagnetist
Interprets the fossil evidence in rocks and sediments from continents and oceans to record the spreading of the seabed and continental drift.

Seismologist
Monitors earthquakes and the shock waves they produce in the earth.

Visit the museum of science, art, and human perception and interact with the earthquake exhibits.
The Exploratorium Learning Studio
3601 Lyon Street
San Francisco, CA 94123
Phone: (415) 561-0399
www.exploratorium.edu/

See exciting earthquake features at the Earth Galleries of the Natural History Museum.
Natural History Museum
London SW7 5BD, England
Phone: 44 0 20 7942 5000
www.nhm.ac.uk/visit-us/galleries

A spectacular flow
of lava pours
from a volcano

CHAPTER 2

Volcanoes

A volcanic eruption is one of the natural world's most awe-inspiring events. Huge clouds of suffocating ash, rivers of scalding lava, lumps of molten rock hurled through the air, and catastrophic explosions are some of the deadly results of eruptions. Volcanoes that erupt regularly are called active volcanoes, and most are close to the earth's weak spots at the boundaries of the tectonic plates. The name volcano comes from Vulcan, the ancient Roman god of fire (in the past people believed that angry gods lived inside of volcanoes). Living in the shadow of a volcano can be extremely dangerous. However, many people do, because volcanic soil is very fertile. Volcanic eruptions have caused some of the worst disasters in history. It has been estimated that more than one million people have died as a result of volcanic activity in the past 2,000 years. Some historians believe that volcanoes have even been responsible for destroying several ancient civilizations.

Eruption!

Volcanoes are openings in the earth. During an eruption magma, or molten rock, makes its way upward from deep inside the mantle, as far as 99 miles (160km) below the earth's surface. The magma, mixed with gases, bursts through the crust and flows out as lava. Rock, ash, steam, and hot gases may erupt with it. The lava eventually cools down and solidifies around the vent, sometimes forming a volcano's familiar cone shape.

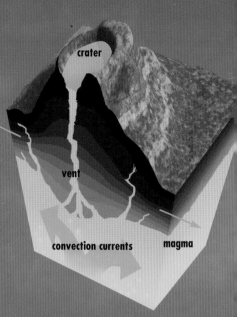

▶ A volcano erupts when magma inside the magma chamber below the volcano builds up enough pressure to rise up through the vent. Currents called convection currents, along with the movement of tectonic plates, can produce cracks in the crust where a volcano forms.

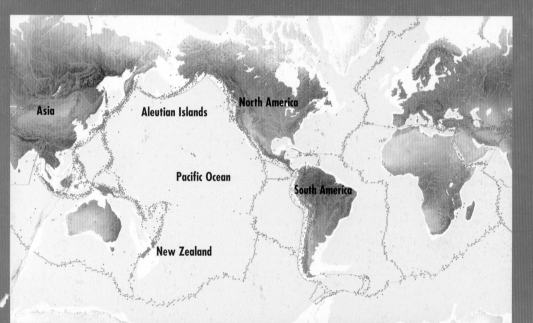

▲ Most volcanoes (red dots) are found along the boundaries between the earth's tectonic plates (gray lines). Around the Pacific Ocean is the Ring of Fire—a great arc that stretches from New Zealand, along the eastern edge of Asia, north across the Aleutian Islands of Alaska, and south along the coasts of North and South America. Almost 75 percent of the world's volcanoes are found there. It is located at the edges of the Pacific plate and other tectonic plates.

Cracks and hot spots

The majority of volcanoes occur along the cracks in the lithosphere that mark the edges of the world's tectonic plates. These are the weakest spots in the earth's surface. There are, however, some eruptions in the middle of plates (such as Kilauea, Hawaii, which is a long way from the edge). The places where these occur are called hot spots. Scientists believe that they are made by thin plumes of very hot magma that rise up and punch holes in the plate.

Types of volcanoes

Volcanoes come in different shapes, depending on the type of eruption. Shield volcanoes have shallow, sloping sides and are formed by very hot, runny lava that spreads over a wide area. Cone-shaped volcanoes result from thick layers of volcanic ash and cinders that erupt from a central crater. More explosive eruptions create broad craters called calderas.

uilding and destroying

volcano, like other violent natural forces, can transform a
ndscape beyond recognition. It can create land with its lava,
ven giving birth to new islands out at sea. It can form vast
nderground tunnels, as well as dramatic shapes where the
va cools, including ledges, pillars and domes. And, of course,
volcano can also obliterate a landscape, smothering it with
ed-hot rock and ash, or blasting it with superheated gases.

▶ The island of Surtsey,
southwest of Iceland, rose
out of the sea in a single day
in 1963. It was created by a
volcanic eruption of lava on
the seabed. Within two years
Surtsey was 590 feet high
and 1.5 miles across.

◤ Magma, or liquefied rock,
merges from a volcano's
ater as lava. The steep sides
this volcano in Montserrat
ave been formed by thick
va cooling and hardening
fore it has had a chance to
read very far.

▼ A red-hot river of lava engulfs a house on Heimaey, an island off Iceland, during the long eruption of 1973. Ash and lava flows forced people to abandon the island's only town.

Buried by lava

In June 1783 a series of earthquakes shook Mount Skaptar in Iceland—a country that has more than 180 volcanoes. A fissure, or crack, opened up in the Laki volcano on the side of the mountain. Out of it poured a flood of lava, which kept flowing for five long months. By the end of the year lava covered a large part of the country, burying many villages and fields. The lava flows were so hot that they melted nearby glaciers, causing extensive flooding across the country.

◀ The bodies of people buried by ash from Mount Vesuvius decomposed, leaving hollow casts. When these were filled with plaster 1,800 years later, the victims were revealed.

▶ Pahoehoe lava can easily outrun a person. This runny lava solidifies into smooth, unusual shapes and is sometimes called lava sculpture.

▶ Thicker lava, which moves slower and cools with a thick skin, is called "aa" lava. This breaks up to form jagged and twisted rock.

▶ Very hot, fluid lava flows from Kilauea volcano on the island of Hawaii. When the lava reaches the sea, it cools to form solid rock.

From liquid to rock

When lava leaves the volcano's vent, it is a liquid that can reach temperatures as high as 2,192°F (1,200°C). Lava can flow many miles before it starts to cool down. Eventually it hardens into rock. But its final shape and texture can vary, depending on how hot it was when it emerged from the volcano.

Poison from the sky

Lava scorches and buries everything in its path. Volcanoes can also produce other deadly substances. The Laki eruption released vast clouds of poisonous fumes from the vent that hung over the landscape for several months. This killed off sheep, cattle, and crops and caused a famine that eventually wiped out one fifth of the population of Iceland.

Roman tragedy

In August A.D. 79 Mount Vesuvius in Italy erupted. Pyroclastic flows, made up of hot gas, ash, and molten rock, exploded out of the volcano. People in the nearby town of Pompeii suffocated or burned to death. On the other side of the mountain the town of Herculaneum disappeared under a deluge of mud and ash.

▼ Following the eruption in June 1991 of Mount Pinatubo in the Philippines, nearby towns and villages were covered in a thick carpet of ash.

Exploding volcanoes

A volcano generates a staggering amount of energy. In many eruptions this energy is released as the lava and gases flow out. But imagine if the energy cannot escape. What if the lava moves so slowly that it blocks the vent? The intense heat and the gas pressure build up inside the volcano until there is only one possible result— the volcano is blown apart in a gigantic explosion.

▲ Islanders watch as clouds of ash emerge from Mount Pelée in May 1902. Despite this warning sign that the volcano was about to erupt, most people did not evacuate.

▲ When Mount Pelée erupted, fire and the force of the explosion reduced the town of St. Pierre to rubble. One of the two survivors was a prisoner in the town's jail.

▼ Trees flattened by the blast from Mount St. Helens in 1980 cover the surface of nearby Spirit Lake. It has been estimated that the eruption released the equivalent amount of energy to 27,000 atomic bombs of the type that was dropped on Hiroshima.

Caribbean tragedy
Early in 1902 Mount Pelée, on the Caribbean island of Martinique, began to grow. The volcano, which lay at the top of the mountain, had been plugged by a buildup of lava. Over the next few months this pushed itself skyward in a rocky spike, until it was 1,968 feet (600m) above the crater. On May 8 the mountain exploded and expelled a searing blast of very hot gas. In only three minutes the nearby town of St. Pierre was completely destroyed. Out of the population of 28,000 people, there were only two survivors.

Deadly cloud
The cloud of gas, ash, and rock fragments from the Mount Pelée eruption traveled at 108 feet (33m) per second, leaving no time for escape. After burning the town, it rolled out to sea and set fire to ships. One eyewitness described how "the side of the volcano was ripped out, and there hurled straight toward us a solid wall of flame . . . it was like a hurricane of fire." Scientists now describe this type of extreme volcanic eruption as a pyroclastic flow. The 1902 disaster was widely reported across the world and made people much more aware of the dangers posed by active volcanoes.

Volcano watch
Today scientists closely monitor the behavior of active volcanoes. Satellite technology, such as the Global Positioning System (GPS), is used to make frequent measurements of a mountain's shape in order to detect any changes. When magma rises to the surface, it may cause the top of the mountain to bulge—a sign that a volcano might erupt. In 1980 scientists identified such a bulge on Mount St. Helens, Washington. The area was cleared, and two months later the volcano exploded. Although 57 people died, the death toll would have been much higher without the early warning.

▲ Mount St. Helens had been dormant for more than 100 years, when it exploded with catastrophic results in May 1980. The nine-hour eruption destroyed all living things within an area of around 70 square miles, and volcanic ash rained down on eleven U.S. states. Glaciers on the mountain melted and triggered lahars, or volcanic mudslides. The top of the mountain disintegrated, reducing its height from 9,676 feet to 8,364 feet and forming a one-mile-wide horseshoe-shaped crater. Mount St. Helens is still active today, more than 25 years later.

After the eruption

A volcanic eruption can bring devastation to the surrounding area within a few minutes. But volcanoes can also have an impact on distant places and may even change weather patterns around the world. When a volcano exploded on the tiny Indonesian island of Krakatoa on August 27, 1883, it could be heard from as far as southern Australia, more than 1,984 miles (3,200km) away. The explosion destroyed most of the island, but worse was still to come. The volcano collapsed into the sea, triggering tsunamis that could be felt as far away as South Africa

Blotting out the sun

The explosion on Krakatoa also blasted a huge cloud of ash more than 50 miles (80km) into the sky. It was so dense that the region around the island suffered from two days of total darkness. Crops and vegetation in Java and Sumatra were destroyed by the ash falls. Air currents carried the cloud around the earth several times, and the light reflecting on the countless dust particles created a series of brightly colored sunsets in Europe and North America.

▲ This historical print shows a cloud of ash emerging from Krakatoa during the early stages of its eruption in 1883. The main island was destroyed in the explosion, but today there are four small islands covered in forests on the site.

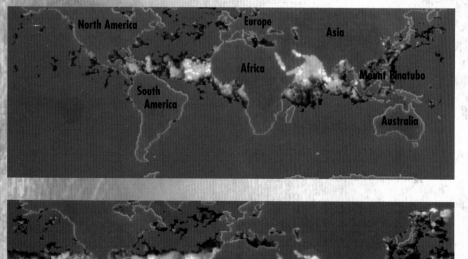

◀ A satellite picture that was taken soon after the eruption of Mount Pinatubo in the Philippines in 1991 highlights the spreading of airborne particles, or aerosols, that were released high into the atmosphere.

◀ Eight weeks later the cloud of aerosols had spread across the planet. As well as causing very red sunrises and sunsets, the cloud reflected some of the sun's heat back into space, lowering the earth's temperature by a few degrees.

flood of mud

s well as tsunamis, there are other dangers that occur
hen volcanoes and water meet. If there is heavy rainfall
ter an eruption, the combination of ash and rain can
eate a river of mud, which races down the mountainside,
urying everything below. In 1919 a mudflow at the Kelut
olcano in Java left 5,500 people dead. Another threat
omes from the lakes that sometimes form in volcanic
aters. If a lake fractures in an eruption, its contents can
roduce a massive mudflow.

▼ A telephone booth is buried in
mud, along with the rest of the
town of Plymouth, on the Caribbean
island of Montserrat after the
eruption of Mount Soufriere in
1997. The intense sunset, caused
by the scattering of volcanic dust, is
called volcanic twilight.

The end of a civilization

Major eruptions can sometimes change the course of history.
More than 3,000 years ago the Minoan people of Crete were
the most powerful people in the Mediterranean. In 1650 B.C.,
however, Thera volcano on the island of Santorini, 43 miles
(70km) to the south of Crete, was shattered by a powerful
eruption. This set off a tsunami, possibly 100 feet (30m) in
height, that smashed into the north and east coasts of
Crete. Some historians now believe that this brought the
great Minoan civilization to a dramatic end.

Sleeping giants

There are at least 500 active volcanoes across the planet that erupt regularly. Every year an average of 50 actually erupt. Fortunately, most of them happen in places where few or no people live, such as the seabed, and, as a result, many go unnoticed. However, a few bring disasters. The highest death tolls tend to occur in less developed countries, where there are no volcano warning systems and communications are basic.

▲ This spectacular aerial view shows a hot spring in Yellowstone National Park, U.S. It is heated by underground volcanic activity and is just one indication of a supervolcano below the surface.

◄ In 1994 scientists sent this robot into the crater of Mount Spurr, Alaska. It was designed to study the interior of this active volcano and take gas samples and video images.

Studying volcanoes

Although we have sent spacecraft millions of miles into space, it is much more difficult to explore more than a few miles below the earth's surface. Because of the high temperatures, the current limit for drills and other testing equipment is around six miles (9km). Magma and other volcanic materials come from much deeper than this. Volcanologists—the scientists who study volcanoes—do most of their work on the surface, observing lava flows and pyroclastic outbursts.

ose to the action

 keep track of underground activity,
ientists have to rely on a combination of
story and science. The history of a volcano
n sometimes be traced back hundreds of
ars and will show how it might behave
 the future. Volcanologists can also use
struments to measure tiny movements
elow the surface and to track changes in the
mperature, magnetism, and electrical charge
 the magma. Volcanologists often work on the
ry edge of a crater, and this can put them into
ositions of great danger. A number of volcanologists
ave lost their lives in recent years, including three who
ere killed by a pyroclastic cloud at Mount Unzen in Japan.

upervolcano

ensitive instruments have revealed a "supervolcano"—an
normous lake of magma—below Yellowstone National Park
 the U.S. The ground there frequently swells and subsides. If
e magma bursts through the crust, the resulting explosion
ould be 10,000 times more powerful than the Mount St.
elens eruption and cause a global catastrophe.

▶ A volcanologist, close to the vent of Mount Etna in
Sicily, Italy, films the eruption of 2002. He is protected
from the intense heat by a full thermal suit.

SUMMARY OF CHAPTER 2: VOLCANOES

Erupting lava

Volcanoes usually occur at the edges of tectonic plates. Some volcanoes, however, are found at hot spots, which are located in the middle of the earth's plates. During a volcanic eruption molten rock, called magma, forces its way up from deep below the surface. The magma, mixed with gases, pushes through a vent, or opening, and flows out as lava. Ash, steam, and gas clouds may erupt with it. The lava eventually cools and solidifies as rock. Solidified lava can take on different appearances, depending on the temperature of the lava when it left the volcano.

Explosive volcanoes

If a volcano's vent becomes blocked by lava, there can be a buildup of gas and intense heat. This can result in a violent explosion of molten rock, ash, and hot gas. This type of eruption is called a pyroclastic flow and can cause complete devastation in the vicinity. Volcanic eruptions can also have a huge impact on places that are much farther away. They can create tsunamis, which flood coasts thousands of miles away. The giant ash clouds blasted out during an eruption can reach high up into the atmosphere and reduce the sun's heating effect on the earth. This can result in a lowering of global temperatures. The ash can also mix with water to form deadly mudflow.

A plaster cast of one of the victims of Mount Vesuvius, which erupted in A.D. 79, burying Pompeii and Herculaneum in ash

Volcanologists at work

There are at least 500 volcanoes throughout the world that are active and might erupt. On average, around 50 of these erupt each year. Scientists called volcanologists perform vital work studying the behavior of volcanoes. They take measurements, such as the temperature below the surface, and monitor underground movements in order to keep track of active volcanoes. A volcano's history can also provide clues that help volcanologists predict eruptions.

Go further . . .

For tips about predicting eruptions, interactive games, and video clips, visit: www.learner.org/exhibits/volcanoes

Discover more about active volcanoes around the world at: volcano.und.nodak.edu

Read about Jupiter's highly volcanic moon, Io, at: www.nineplanets.org/io.html

The Volcano Adventure Guide by Rosaly Lopes (Cambridge University Press, 2005)

Volcanoes: Fire from the Earth by Maurice Krafft (Gardner Books, 1993)

Astrogeologist
Studies surface conditions and features on moons and planets.

Geochemist
Specializes in the study of the earth's composition, analyzing rock, soil, and gases.

Geomorphologist
Investigates the origin of landforms and the processes that shape them.

Igneous petrologist
Investigates how magma cools and forms different types of lava.

Volcanologist
Studies volcanoes and helps predict volcanic eruptions.

See Mount St. Helens, and, if the conditions are right, climb to the crater rim.
Visitor Center, Mount St. Helens
3029 Spirit Lake Highway
Castle Rock, WA 98611
Phone: (360) 274-0962
www.fs.fed.us/gpnf/mshnvm/

Experience one of Europe's most active volcanoes, Mount Etna, in Sicily, Italy. You can arrange a guided tour and learn more about the volcano at the visitor's center.
Via Etnea
Sicily, Italy
Phone: 1 39 95 914588

An approaching tornado in South Dakota

CHAPTER 3

Storms, floods, and snow

arthquakes and volcanoes begin deep beneath the earth. Other natural azards come from above the planet's surface in the form of weather. From a eavy snowfall that can start an avalanche a ferocious hurricane hitting a coastal wn, the world's weather is governed by ree simple elements—water, air, and eat. The heat of the sun evaporates ater from the oceans, turning it into visible water vapor. Warm air rises, so e water vapor is carried up into the sky.

Eventually it reaches a colder region of air, where it turns into tiny droplets that form clouds. But just as warm air rises, cold air sinks. These forces moving in opposite directions produce winds and air currents. The winds and the clouds produce all types of extreme weather conditions across the world, including severe thunderstorms and tornadoes. Storms often bring heavy rainfall that can cause rivers to burst their banks, flooding huge areas of land.

Danger in the air

The atmosphere is a layer of air that is wrapped around our planet. It protects us from the sun's harmful radiation and helps keep the earth warm. The atmosphere extends upward from the surface for around 620 miles (1,000km), but the world's weather takes place in the lowest and smallest part. This is called the troposphere, which reaches around six miles (10km) into the sky. There the air is always moving, carrying heat and moisture around the globe. Too much movement can generate giant storms that cause devastation in the form of tornadoes, hurricanes, and floods.

▲ This satellite image shows the earth's cloud cover in three dimensions. Many of these clouds will bring severe storms, accompanied by lightning, thunder, hail, and heavy rain.

What is wind?

Wind is air that moves in a horizontal direction (air that moves vertically is called a current). Winds are created by the uneven heating of the earth by the sun. Warm air rises, and cold air rushes in to take its place. When this air blows across the land, features such as mountains, hills, and woodlands often slow it down. These obstacles break up the wind into gusts and eddies, known as air turbulence. These do not often pose a great danger. When wind blows across the sea, however, it travels much faster, pulling up heat and moisture from the water.

▶ This storm over Kansas is a supercell thunderstorm. These storms, which produce torrential rain and hail, are at their most destructive when they remain over one area for an extended period of time. Supercell storms often develop into tornadoes.

orm birth

he weather acts as a type of safety valve for
e earth, preventing any one area of the world
om getting too hot or too cold. It works by
ifting hot air to cold places and cold air to
ot places. The warmest part of the world
the tropical region on both sides of the
quator. This produces a huge amount of hot
nd moist air, which rises and then flows
ward the North and South poles, where the
r is the coldest. This movement of air restores
e balance of heat in the atmosphere, but it
n also trigger storms by creating very strong
inds and massive storm clouds that drop rain,
ail, or snow. Most storms begin life where the
inds are the strongest of all—over the ocean.

▲ Force-12 winds can overturn light aircraft and even toss them into trees. These two were
destroyed by Hurricane Gilbert, which struck Kingston, Jamaica, in September 1988.

The Beaufort scale

In 1805 Francis Beaufort, a captain in the British Royal
Navy, devised a system for judging the speed of the wind.
A modified version is still used today, and it is known as the
Beaufort scale. At one end of the scale is force 0 ("calm"),
where there is almost no wind and smoke rises vertically.
Halfway along the scale is force 6 ("strong breeze"), where
winds reach 31mph (50km/h), small trees sway, and telegraph
wires whistle. Near gale, gale, strong gale, and severe gale
follow. When wind speeds hit 63mph (102km/h), force 11
("violent storm") has been reached. Trees may be flattened
and cars overturned. Force 12 is in progress when the winds
exceed 74mph (120km/h). This is classified as a hurricane—
buildings are destroyed, and there may be loss of life.

◀ Scientists from the Severe Thunderstorm Electrification
and Precipitation Study (STEPS) get ready to launch a
weather balloon into the storm cloud. The balloon carries
instruments that record temperature, wind speed, air
pressure, and the electrical charges inside a storm.

▶ Flying debris is a major hazard when a hurricane hits the coast. Hurricanes, which draw their energy from the sea, lose their power as they move inland.

Hurricane alert

Hurricanes are the planet's most ferocious storms. Known as cyclones in Australia and typhoons in southeast Asia, they bring with them massive waves and wind speeds that can gust up to 186mph (300km/h). Almost all hurricanes are formed in the warm waters of the tropics. Each year southeast and southern Asia are battered by more than 30 hurricanes. The hurricane season also brings death and devastation to southern parts of the U.S. and Central America.

Birth of a hurricane

A hurricane is made up of bands of thunderclouds that spin around a clear, still center called the eye. Winds blowing across the warm seas close to the equator suck up heat and water vapor to form the storms that produce hurricanes. The swirling mass of thunderclouds is set spinning by the rotation of the earth and by winds from the poles. A hurricane can last for weeks and travel many thousands of miles.

▼ This satellite picture shows Hurricane Ivan over the Caribbean Sea in September 2004. When it struck Grenada, more than three quarters of the island's homes were badly damaged.

Landfall

Over the ocean hurricanes are a threat to ships, but when they reach land, the dangers are even greater. The strength of the wind can tear down trees and flatten buildings. As well as whipping up massive waves, hurricanes can also cau a rise in the ocean level, or storm surge which can drive the sea far inland.

Hurricane Katrina

Hurricane Katrina hit the U.S. on August 29, 2005. Winds of 140mph (225km/h) created a 30-foot (9m) storm surge. Water breached the dykes that protected the city of New Orleans and flooded the low-lying coastlines of Louisiana, Alabama, and Mississippi. With the damage estimated at more than $200 million, and more than one million people forced to leave their homes, Katrina is the most expensive and most destructive natural disaster in U.S. history.

▶ Hurricane Andrew, which struck Florida in August 1992, was one of the most powerful hurricanes of the last 100 years. More than 100,000 homes were badly damaged, and many residential areas, such as this trailer park, were flattened.

Twisters

When a tornado descends from a storm cloud and touches down on land, it can leave a terrible trail of destruction in its wake. The Tri-State Twister, which ripped through the U.S. states of Missouri, Illinois, and Indiana in 1925, demolished nine towns and killed almost 700 people. A tornado's path is almost impossible to predict. One house in a street might be flattened, while the neighboring houses are left untouched. Twisters have also been known to suck up the water from rivers and even lift trains from their tracks.

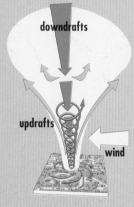

downdrafts

updrafts

wind

▲ Tornadoes form when warm, rising air, called the updraft, is set spinning by winds blowing from the side.

Born from a storm

Tornadoes, like hurricanes, are violent winds that spiral around a still center. They are formed during severe thunderstorms and are often accompanied by severe lightning and hail. Unlike a hurricane, a tornado's life span is much shorter—usually only a few minutes—and its base can be as narrow as 164 feet (50m) in diameter. The spinning winds, which cause most of the damage, can reach an incredible 310mph (500km/h).

◀ The furiously spinning winds of a tornado can car cars and other objects throu the air. People and cattle ha been lifted from the grou and dropped hundreds of f away. Even weak twisters h enough power to rip roofs houses and overturn cars.

ender pressure

ornado damage can also be caused by differences in the ir pressure. This happens when the speed of the wind owers the air pressure on the outside surface of a house. he air pressure inside stays the same, which means that is higher than on the outside, causing the house to xplode. The roof lifts up, and the side walls blow out. ngineers have not yet found a way of constructing building that will stand up to this sort of treatment.

▲ Tornadoes are common in Bangladesh, where powerful thunderstorms develop at the beginning of the monsoon season in April and May. In 1989 a tornado killed an estimated 1,300 people. The loss of life is often high because buildings are poorly constructed and the region is densely populated.

Across the world

There are around 1,000 tornadoes each year in the U.S. Most of them occur in the area known as Tornado Alley, which includes the states of Nebraska, Kansas, Oklahoma, and Texas. There, warm, moist air from the Gulf of Mexico meets cold, dry air from the Rockies, creating ideal conditions for the formation of twisters. Less violent tornadoes, however, also happen in many other countries, including Bangladesh, South Africa, Japan, and the United Kingdom.

◣ This distinctive cloud formation, called "mammatus," hangs from the underside of a storm cloud Alberta, Canada. It is often a sign that a very severe thunderstorm or tornado is on its way.

Danger at sea

▲ A waterspout is a tornado that forms over water. Although rarer and less violent than twisters, waterspouts can pose a danger to shipping.

More than 200 supertankers and giant container vessels have sunk because of severe weather in the last 20 years. Rogue, or freak, waves, which can reach heights of up to 100 feet (30m) (as high as a 12-story building), were probably responsible for many of the losses. Although rogue waves are rare, many people have experienced these terrifying monsters. In 1995 an offshore oil platform in the North Sea was hit by a wave that measured 85 feet (26m) in height. The cruise ship *Queen Elizabeth II* survived one that was just as big one month later, and other ships have been damaged by even taller waves.

Freak waves

Rogue waves were once believed to be the stuff of legends. However, recent studies, using data from satellites and radar, have proved their existence beyond any doubt. At one site in the North Sea 466 rogue waves were recorded over a period of twelve years. In 2000 the European Union set up a project called MaxWave to monitor the seas and learn more about these waves. The findings of this project are now being used to improve the design of ships.

◄ One of the most famous prints by the Japanese artist Hokusai, from around 1830, shows a huge wave threatening some boats below. Mount Fuji can be seen in the background. During severe storms, waves, whipped up by the wind, can reach heights of 50 feet or more.

◀ A giant wave crashes into a lighthouse outside a harbor on France's Atlantic coast in November 2000. The storm was so severe that an around-the-world yacht race was postponed for three days.

Unstable waves

Some scientists believe that rogue waves, which occur far out at sea, form when two strong currents meet. The currents push together, building up waves that are much taller than normal. It has also been suggested that some storm waves can become unstable when they are moving at high speeds. When this happens, the unstable wave sucks in energy from other local waves and may increase its size very quickly. Some of these giant waves have been known to come in groups of three.

▼ A fishing boat is dwarfed by a giant wave in a scene from the movie *The Perfect Storm* (2000). The title refers to the ideal conditions that combined to create a fierce storm that hit the east coast of North America in 1991.

Waterspouts

Waterspouts are spinning funnels of air that can pull up water from a lake or sea to heights of up to 2,952 feet (900m). Unlike tornadoes, they do not need a storm cloud in order to form. Waterspouts rarely last longer than 15 minutes. Most waterspouts occur in the warm waters of the tropics, but they have also been known to form in cooler climates. In December 1879 three waterspouts slammed into the Tay Bridge in Scotland. The bridge was already weakened by gales, and the waterspouts caused a large section to collapse, just as a train was crossing. The train plunged into the river below, killing 75 people.

▼ This print shows rescue boats searching for bodies among the wreckage from the train that fell into the River Tay, Scotland, when a bridge collapsed after it was hit by a cluster of waterspouts.

Floods

Floods are the deadliest of all natural disasters. They have been a feature of many myths and religious writings since recorded history began. Almost one half of all disaster victims die from drowning or from the effects of flooding, such as starvation (when crops are ruined) and diseases, like dysentery and typhoid, which thrive in the water. There are many natural causes of flooding, including hurricanes, torrential rains, and tsunamis. Unfortunately, many people live in places that are at risk of being flooded. Around one half of the world's population has their homes close to rivers or on low coastal land.

▲ When the Chang, or Yangtze, river overflowed in August 1998 the Chinese government evacuated hundreds of thousands of people One third of China's 1.2 billion people live in the Chang river valle

Bangladesh disaster

Bangladesh suffers from the misery of floods from two directions. Meltwater roars down the great rivers from the Himalayan mountains, while hurricanes (known as cyclones in this region) cause storm surges that overrun the low-lying shores. This tragic pattern has been repeated many times. Catastrophic floods killed two million people in 1970. The storms of 1998 brought more misery and made millions of people homeless.

China's Sorrow

China also experiences flooding on a huge scale. The Chang, or Yangtze, river, known as "China's Sorrow," carries a rich load of silt that creates very fertile land on the plains, and many farmers grow crops there. Over hundreds of years they have built up dykes to hold back the water during the wet season, but the river has frequently broken through. More than two million people died in the floods in 1887.

▼ Torrential rainfall deluged western India in July 2005. The resulting floods devastated the city of Mumbai and affected 20 million people in the region. Below, people hold onto a rope as they cross a street that has been sumberged by the floodwater.

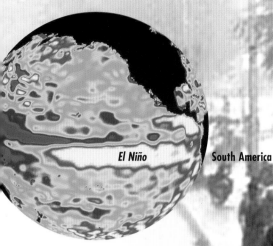

El Niño   South America

This satellite image shows the current of warm water
[call]ed *El Niño*. Every five to seven years it heads toward
[Sout]h America, bringing heavy rainfall and flooding.

▲ In 1953 low-lying coastal areas of the Netherlands
and eastern England were devastated by severe flooding.

high risk

[So]me coastlines are sinking, putting them
[at] high risk of flooding. This has been
[ha]ppening for hundreds of years to parts of
[so]utheast England and the Netherlands. In
[Ja]nuary 1953 a storm roared down the east
[co]ast of England, building up a huge bank
[of] water. The storm surge came at the
[sa]me time as a very high tide, breaching
[th]e seawalls. Thousands of homes were
[de]stroyed, and more than 2,000 people
[dr]owned in England and the Netherlands.

Avalanches

In May 1970 a powerful earthquake shook the Andes mountains in Peru. The ice cap from the summit of Peru's highest peak, Mount Huascarán, shattered, sending thousands of tons of rock smashing onto a glacier. A 262-foot (80m)-high wall of snow, ice, rock, and mud hurtled down the mountainside at more than 198mph (320km/h). Within four minutes the avalanche had buried the ski resort of Yungay. At least 25,000 people died in this disaster.

▲ These rescue workers are training to locate avalanche victims, using long rods called probes. The incredible weight of the snow makes it almost impossible for people trapped in an avalanche to dig their way out.

Triggers

A buildup of snow on the upper slopes of a mountain can become a lethal avalanche—especially if the snow on the lower slopes becomes unstable because of heavy rain. Without adequate support, a giant slab of snow and ice can break free and sweep down the mountainside. Avalanches can be set off by a variety of events, including a strong wind, a change in temperature, or a skier going down a slope.

▲ The force of an avalanche has completely crushed these cars. Heavy snowfall combined with a rise in temperature triggered this avalanche.

◀ An avalanche roars down a mountainside, collecting rocks and trees that add to its destructive power. An avalanche can also generate high-speed winds, called the "sigh of the avalanche," that flatten trees and buildings.

Alpine disaster

Every year around 100 people are killed by avalanches in the European Alps. The winter of 1998 to 1999 was particularly deadly because of unusually heavy snowfall in the region. Some areas had up to six times more snow than the average, creating ideal conditions for avalanches. On February 24, 1999, a huge slab of snow, 328 feet (100m) high and weighing more than 200,000 tons, broke away from a mountainside in Austria and smashed into the village of Galtür. In less than one minute the village disappeared under a 26-foot (8m)-thick blanket of snow, and more than 30 people lost their lives.

Avalanche survival

If you are caught in an avalanche, you only have a one in twenty chance of survival. Many victims are killed by the sheer force of the falling snow or ice. If they survive this and are buried in the snow, they need to be rescued within 15 minutes. After this time they will run out of air to breathe and suffer from hypothermia (loss of body heat). Rescuers use heat detectors, sound detectors, and radars to locate people who are trapped under snow, as well as the much more traditional method of specially trained dogs.

▼ Rescue workers sift through the area that has been flooded by the overflow from the Vaiont dam in northern Italy in October 1963, after a massive rock slide crashed into the lake. Almost 2,000 people living in the valley drowned. Before the dam was built, engineers had pointed out that there was a high risk of landslides in the region.

Fighting back

Meteorologists have a wide range of tools to make short-range and long-range weather forecasts and to monitor the progress of extreme weather conditions. These include weather balloons, launched several times a day to measure wind and temperatures, and satellite images that reveal the telltale cloud spirals of a hurricane forming over the ocean. This information can be used to alert people about severe weather far in advance so that they can take any necessary action.

Tracking storms

Radar has proved to be one of the most effective instruments for forecasting. Weather-radar networks scan the skies, sending out pulses of radio waves. These bounce back when they meet a target, such as raindrops, snow, or hail, enabling meteorologists to build up a detailed image of weather systems. Doppler radar, which measures changes in the returning echoes, can even help predict the formation of tornadoes.

▲ In this experiment lightning in a thundercloud is artificially triggered by a rocket. Attached to the rocket is a copper wire, which provides a path for the lightning to reach instruments that are on the surface. The experiment provides scientists with a better understanding of the processes that produce violent storms.

▶ This special truck is equipped with Doppler radar, which can detect the direction and speed of a violent storm. It can help weather forecasters identify where hail, heavy rainfall, and tornadoes are likely to form.

Avalanche defense

As well as using effective warning systems, there are other ways that we can protect ourselves from some hazards. In areas that are at risk from avalanches, for example, series of wedge-shaped barriers that are constructed from metal or concrete to divert an avalanche away from houses. Sometimes small-scale avalanches, which pose no threat to people, are deliberately started with explosives to clear away a potentially dangerous buildup of snow.

▲ A radar-equipped airplane flies right into the heart of a storm. The long probe at the front contains instruments that take readings such as measuring turbulence. The airplane is nicknamed Snoopy. Information from research aircraft is combined with data from weather stations on the ground in order to help track the development of storms.

The threat of climate change

The earth's climate has always been changing. However, as a result of human behavior—especially the burning of large amounts of fossil fuels—global temperatures have risen significantly over the last one hundred years. This has caused glaciers to retreat and the Arctic ice to get thin. Sea levels have begun to rise, threatening low-lying coasts with devastating floods. Other consequences in the future include the increased risk of droughts in some parts of the world and more severe storms such as hurricanes. Unless we dramatically change the way that we use our available energy resources, natural disasters will inevitably become more frequent.

▼ The Thames Barrier consists of rotating steel gates that are built across a 1,640-foot-wide stretch of the Thames river. When they close, the gates protect London from floods caused by high tides and storms.

DOW3
DOPPLER ON WHEELS

SUMMARY OF CHAPTER 3: STORMS, FLOODS, AND SNOW

Winds

The world's weather occurs in the lowest part of the atmosphere—the blanket of air that surrounds and protects our planet. The sun's heat causes air to rise, and cold air rushes in to take its place. This movement of air produces wind and prevents any single area from getting too hot or too cold. On land the wind is slowed down by hills, mountains, and other features. Out at sea, however, there is nothing to break up the wind, and this is where most violent storms begin.

Hurricanes and tornadoes

A storm with winds of more than 74mph (120km/h) is classified as a hurricane. Hurricanes are formed when strong winds pull up heat and water vapor from the warm seas close to the

The rapidly rotating funnel of a waterspout, with spray at its base, near Cyprus in the eastern part of the Mediterranean Sea

equator. This generates a mass of thunderclouds that is set spinning by the earth's rotation. When hurricanes hit the land, the violent winds often bring destruction to a wide area. Hurricanes can be accompanied by storm surge that sweep the sea inland, causing widespread flooding. Tornadoes are much smaller spinning storms, formed over land during severe thunderstorms. Although most twisters only last a few minutes, their ferocious wind speeds of up to 310mph (500km/h) can be deadly in populated areas.

The impact of floods

Floods kill more people than any other type of disaster. Ther are many natural causes of flooding, including storm surge created by hurricanes, torrential rains, and tsunamis. Man people live in places with a high risk of flooding, such as low lying coasts and river valleys, where the land is often very ferti and good for farming. Climate change, worsened by humar activity, such as the burning of fossil fuels, has raised the leve of the ocean and made floods even more likely in the future

Go further . . .

Visit the official site of the U.S. National Hurricane Center at: www.nhc.noaa.gov

Explore every aspect of the weather and climate at: www.metoffice.co.uk

Find out what storm chasers do and join them as they track wild weather at: www.stormchaser.com

Eyewitness: Hurricane and Tornado by Jack Challoner (Dorling Kindersley, 2004)

Raging Floods (Awesome Forces of Nature) by Louise A. Spilsbury and Richard Spilsbury (Heinemann, 2003)

Civil engineer
An engineer who designs and builds public structures, including dams and flood prevention schemes.

Climatologist
Specializes in the history of the planet's climate over hundreds or even millions of years.

Meteorologist
Studies the earth's atmosphere and makes predictions about the weather.

Storm chaser
Tracks down storms, including hurricanes and tornadoes to photograph or study them.

Visit the Weather Gallery to see a fantastic working model of a twister.
The Weather Gallery
The National Center for Atmospheric Research (NCAR)
1850 Table Mesa Drive
Boulder, CO 80305
Phone: (303) 497-1174
www.eo.ucar.edu/visit/

Visit the Thames Barrier at:
The Thames Barrier
Learning Centre
London SE18 5JN, England
Phone: 44 0 20 8305 4188

CHAPTER 4

Droughts, fires, and diseases

Earthquakes, storms, and many other natural hazards usually happen over a relatively short period of time. Even the most destructive hurricane loses its power after a few days. There are other natural disasters, however, that can last for years—even decades. Their effects may be so devastating that a full recovery is not possible. Drought, caused by lower-than-average rainfall, is a long-term threat in very arid places, bringing famine, poverty, and illnesses connected to malnutrition.

Where there is little water, there is also the danger of wildfires being started by lightning or by human action. These fires can spread with terrifying speed over huge areas, burning down forests and threatening urban areas. However, an invisible killer is perhaps the deadliest of all. Infectious diseases, such as smallpox and the plague, killed millions of people in the past. Other diseases, such as malaria, have brought sickness and death to some parts of the world for hundreds of years.

▲ Villagers collect water from a well in Gujarat, India, during the severe drought that affected the region in 2003. During a drought people often have to travel incredible distances in order to find supplies of clean drinking water.

▲ A giant dust cloud sweeps across houses in Texas in 1935. During the 1930s drought turned farmland into wasteland, known as the Dust Bowl, from Kansas to New Mexico.

Drought and famine

Humans cannot last for very long without water. Life-giving crops need it in order to grow. If there is not enough water, then plants, animals, and people will die from dehydration or starvation. Large areas of the world suffer from drought, which is mostly caused by lack of rain. Around one third of the earth's land surface is classified as arid, which means that it gets less than ten inches (25cm) c rainfall in one year. The millions of people who live in these arid areas face starvation and death if the rains fail.

Famine in the Sahel

The southern edge of the Sahara desert, called the Sahel, stretches across eight countries in Africa, from Senegal to the Sudan. Since the 1960s the annual rainfall in this desert region has been far below normal. The lack of water for irrigation results in the regular failure of crops. This has led to an almost permanent famine in some areas. In a prolonged drought between 1968 and 1973 as many as 250,000 people and 3.5 million cattle died. Starving families scoured the bare land in a desperate search for wild seeds and corn husks to eat. Since then repeated droughts have created frequent famines—most recently in the south of Niger in 2005.

The increasing desert

Along the northern edge of the Sahara around 390 square miles (1,000km^2) of land becomes desert every year. Below-average rainfall is the main factor, but some scientists believe that it is also caused by the growing population and the demand for food and living space. Grazing cattle and goats eat all the vegetation, and people cut down trees for firewood. This leaves the soil parched and bare, and it reverts to desert that is unable to support people.

Tragedy in China

In poorer nations droughts have taken a terrible toll during the last 100 years. Between 1965 and 1967 starvation caused by droughts resulted in 1.5 million deaths in India, while in Ethiopia in 1984 and 1985 more than one million people lost their lives. The combination of drought and human behavior can also have horrific consequences. During the 1950s China's Communist leader Mao Tse-tung ordered millions of farmers to leave their homes and fields to work in factories. This resulted in massive food shortages. When a drought hit the country at the same time, an estimated 30 to 40 million people died in the famine that resulted.

Wildfires

In hot, dry regions, where the sun parches the vegetation, wildfires can take hold with terrifying speed. Fueled by strong winds, they race across huge distances in North America, parts of Australia, and southern Europe, destroying buildings, trees, and crops. Although wildfires can bring disaster to populated areas, not all their consequences are bad. They can clear away deadwood in forests, leave fertile ash in the soil, and even help germinate the seeds of some trees.

▲ Flames and smoke from wildfires loom above the Simi Valley, California, in October 2003. Fierce, dry winds drove the fires across a wide area, burning many hundreds of houses.

▲ Lightning is the most common cause of wildfires. When lightning strikes the ground, it can heat up the soil to temperatures of up to 3,272°F and instantly set vegetation alight. Some wildfires are deliberately started by people or caused by carelessness such as not putting out campfires.

Bushfires

In the summer searing temperatures and drought provid[e] the ideal conditions for outbreaks of bushfires in parts o[f] Australia, including New South Wales and Victoria. Forest[s] of eucalyptus trees are also found there—their oily bar[k] and leaves are set alight very easily and burn fiercely. Strong winds can blow flaming scraps of bark more than 19 miles (30km), starting dozens of new fires. During bushfires in the Blue Mountains in 2001 firefighters struggled to cope with hundreds of scattered blazes. The fire burned an area twice the size of London, England, an[d] threatened the suburbs of Sydney. Even more disastrou[s] fires in 1983 resulted in the deaths of 72 people.

◄ This specially adapted airplane scoops up water as it flies across a lake and drops it onto fires. Air tankers of this type can also spray chemicals that slow down and cool the flames.

Fighting fire

In areas with a risk from wildfires, surveillance aircraft make regular patrols in the summer and the fall, looking for small fires and observing how they spread. On the ground fire crews may dig trenches called firebreaks to create gaps in the vegetation and try to douse the flames with water, flame-retarding chemicals, or sand. Airplanes can also spray fire retardants and water in an attempt to minimize the spread of the fire. Sometimes, however, only heavy rainfall can quench the flames.

Scorched earth

Wildfires can spread at speeds of up to 14mph (23km/h)—faster than a person can run. Most wildfires burn themselves out quickly, but some can last for weeks, raging across the landscape. The deadliest recorded wildfire broke out close to Peshtigo, Wisconsin, in October 1871. It raced across 2,340 square miles (6,000km²) of parched grass and woodlands, killing 1,500 people on its way. The most expensive wildfire hit Oakland, California, in 1991, destroying houses and causing $1.5 billion worth of damage.

▼ Firefighters on the ground wear protective clothing to shield them from the intense heat of the fire.

Invisible killers

Some of the deadliest natural killers in the world are so tiny that you can only see them through the lens of a microscope. These lethal microorganisms are the bacteria and viruses that spread infectious diseases. They are helped by an army of insects, worms, and other creatures that carry infections from one person to another. Infectious diseases kill millions of people every year across the planet.

Viruses and bacteria

A virus is a simple package of chemicals. But once it gets inside a living cell, it can multiply very quickly, damaging the cell and eventually destroying it. Viruses are the cause of many common illnesses, including measles and chicken pox, as well as life-threatening ones such as polio (poliomyelitis) and SARS (Severe Acute Respiratory Syndrome). Bacteria are also simple organisms. The majority of them are harmless, but some produce deadly diseases, such as cholera, which can spread rapidly.

▲ The schistosome, or bilharzia flatworm, begins life inside water snails and penetrates the skin of humans and other animals. It travels in the bloodstream to the liver and the intestines, causing illness and, frequently, death.

▶ A mosquito pierces a person's skin with its proboscis, or mouthpart, to feed on blood. In this way, it can transmit a parasite called *plasmodium*, which is responsible for malaria. The parasites multiply inside the host's red blood cells before bursting out and infecting even more blood cells. Mosquitoes can also pass on viral diseases such as dengue or yellow fever.

Malaria

◀ The West Nile virus can cause a disease called encephalitis, which inflames the brain. It is transmitted to people and animals by mosquitoes. In 2003 an outbreak of the virus in the U.S. resulted in more than 250 human deaths.

The biggest killer of all is malaria. This is carried by a type of mosquito that passes on the infection when it bites a human and injects the disease into the bloodstream. Victim suffer from a fever and a cold and may then slip into a coma and die. Every year at least 200 million people are affected by malaria, which is very difficult to treat or cure. Around two million of them die. Most victims are children who are living in the tropical and subtropical regions of the world, including central Africa and South America.

▶ Some types of bacteria, such as methicillin-resistant *Staphylococcus aureus*, are resistant to antibiotic drugs. These bacteria cause boils, abscesses, and wound infections, and they can reproduce very quickly.

e war against diseases

ver the last one hundred years doctors and scientists ave developed ways of fighting some of these diseases. r example, they have produced drugs, such as penicillin d other antibiotics, that kill off many types of bacteria. eaner, more hygenic living conditions have also helped the eradication of many infectious diseases in parts of e world. However, in less developed regions diseases ch as malaria, elephantiasis, and sleeping sickness ntinue to have a very strong hold.

▲ A health worker sprays a pesticide in Jakarta, Indonesia, during an outbreak of dengue—a flulike disease that can be fatal. The chemicals inside the spray kill the mosquitoes that transmit dengue.

Pandemic

In October 1347 a fleet of ships arrived at Messina in Sicily, Italy. On board everyone was dying—or already dead. Dark blotches covered the victims' skin, their bodies were swollen, and their tongues were black. Although the sick were prevented from leaving the ships, no one could stop the rats, which were infested with fleas that carried the mystery infection, from scurrying ashore. Soon the people of Messina had the same symptoms as the infected sailors.

▲ The rat flea *Xenopsylla cheopis* carries the bacterium that causes the bubonic plague. The fleas feed off the blood of brown rats and other rats that live close to humans in towns and villages.

The black death

This was the beginning of the black death—one of the first great pandemics, or worldwide epidemics. The disease had been carried along trade routes from China through Russia and the Middle East and then across the Mediterranean. From Messina it spread rapidly through Italy, then raced across Germany, Spain, and France, reaching England in the summer of 1348. Within four years 23 million people had died—around one third of Europe's population.

▼ The black rat, or ship rat, was the major carrier of the plague flea during the black death. Careful control of rats and fleas has rid most of Europe from plague, although it persists in some other parts of the world.

▶ This carved wooden mask was placed as a marker above a burial site for victims of the black death in Rouen, France.

A package of diseases

The black death consisted of three diseases, caused by a bacterium called *Yersina pestis*. The bubonic plague, which killed up to 75 percent of its victims, and septicemic plague, which killed more than 90 percent, were transmitted by fleas. Anyone who caught pneumonic plague, the third disease, was almost certain to die. Pneumonic plague was spread through droplets of saliva when individuals carrying the bacteria coughed and infected other people.

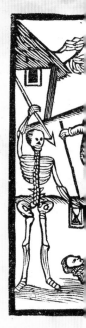

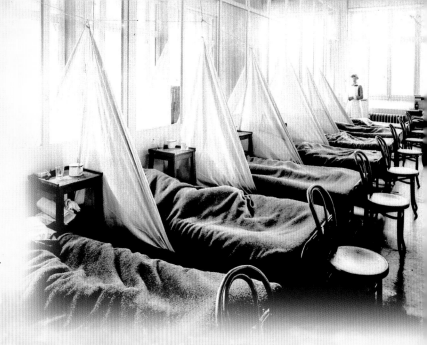

▶ Victims of the 1918 influenza epidemic lie in an army camp hospital in France. The pandemic occurred because a new type of viral infection appeared. Humans had no immunity against this infection, so it spread very quickly, affecting at least one fifth of the world's population.

Return of the plague

The black death faded away in 1351, but other plague epidemics have broken out since. In 1665 a plague killed 100,000 people in London, England. In 1894 there was a major outbreak in China that spread as far as India and the U.S., killing at least ten million people in total. Despite modern medicines, up to 3,000 cases of plague are still recorded across the world each year.

▼ This woodcut represents the coming of the plague to Europe in the 1660s. To the right of the picture is a doctor wearing a beak mask. The beak was filled with strongly scented herbs.

A modern pandemic

One of the deadliest pandemics in history began at the end of World War I in 1918, when a new and deadly strain of influenza appeared. Unlike more common strains of influenza, which usually strike the elderly and newborns, the 1918 flu epidemic targeted the young and healthy, as well as more vulnerable people. Passed from person to person, it swept across the world, and between 25 and 50 million people died.

Defending ourselves

In the war against natural hazards humans do not have the upper hand. There is nothing we can do to prevent hurricanes, droughts, or new diseases from developing. However, we are not completely defenseless. Further research into understanding the causes of these hazards, supported by the use of technology, will continue to make the difference between life and death.

▼ Irrigation systems that channel water to fields allow fertile land to flourish, even in arid conditions.

Dealing with droughts

Scientists now believe that there is a strong link between changes in sea surface temperatures and the periods of low rainfall that result in droughts. More research needs to be done, but in the future accurate drought predictions might be reality.

At a local level measures such as effective crop selection and systems to conserve water are used in drought-prone areas. For example, earth structures, called bunds, stop rainwater from being washed away. Irrigation channels dug into the top of the bunds can also be used to bring water to the crops.

▼ Schoolgirls in Peru wait in line to wash their hands at a new water faucet. Almost three quarters of the world's rural population have no access to clean and fresh water supplies. In many places the water is contaminated with toxic chemicals or sewage.

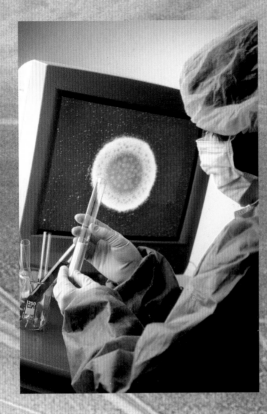

The fight against diseases

The most effective way to fight diseases is to prevent them from taking hold in the first place. The provision of clean drinking water and efficient sewerage (waste water) systems stops germs from breeding and spreading easily. The next crucial step is to make people immune to the diseases. This is done by giving them a vaccine—a mild form of the illness—that will stimulate the body into defending itself against the disease. Vaccinations completely eradicated smallpox after a worldwide campaign during the 1970s.

The planet's most valuable resource

More than one billion people—one in six of the world's population—do not have access to clean drinking water. Almost 6,000 children die every day from diseases that are associated with unsafe water and poor hygiene. Technology can make a real difference, though. This includes filter systems that remove the particles and microbes that are associated with illnesses, such as diarrhea, and solar disinfection, which uses the sun's heat and radiation to make contaminated water clean enough to drink. Until recently people in remote villages in Bangladesh often had to walk for hours in the searing heat to find supplies of water. Now water is piped directly from the hills to many villages by gravity-flow systems. This allows people to collect clean, safe water at any time.

► A child in India is given a polio vaccine by mouth. Polio, which can cause paralysis, can be prevented by giving children the vaccine, which makes them immune to the poliovirus. Vaccination programs have reduced the number of people who are infected with the virus each year from hundreds of thousands to around 1,000.

SUMMARY OF CHAPTER 4: DROUGHTS, FIRES, AND DISEASES

Droughts

Humans depend on water for survival. We need to drink it to stay alive, and it supports the crops that give us food. Many parts of the world, however, suffer from droughts that occur when there is insufficient rainfall. If the crops fail and livestock perish, droughts can also lead to famine. Around one third of the earth's land surface is arid (very dry). Famine is a long-term threat in many arid places—especially for the African countries that lie on the Sahel, the southern edge of the Sahara desert. Some of the

world's deserts, including the Sahara, are increasing in size.

Lightning strikes

Hot, dry regions are at risk from wildfires. Very warm climates create parched vegetation and

Lightning strikes a tree during a powerful storm. If the vegetation is very dry and there are stong winds, a wildfire may start.

strong winds, as well as drying up water sources. In these conditions lightning, as well as human carelessness, can easily start a fire that will spread very quickly. Firefighters deal with these blazes in many ways. These include building firebreaks and using flame-retarding chemicals. Once a wildfire takes hold, however, it can be very difficult to put out. Although wildfires bring great danger, especially in populated areas, they can benefit forests by clearing out dead trees and leaving fertile ash in the soil.

Infectious diseases

Infectious diseases are caused by bacteria and viruses and are responsible for millions of deaths each year. The infections are often carried by hosts—other animals including worms, snails, and insects—which pass them on to humans. An epidemic is caused when an infectious disease quickly spreads among many people. If the disease spreads across the world, it is called a pandemic. The provision of clean water and better living conditions, together with vaccinations and drugs, such as penicillin, have helped combat diseases in many parts of the world.

Go further . . .

 Find out how Australians deal with droughts at: www.bom.gov.au/climate/drought

Learn more about wildfires and see firefighters in action at: www.nifc.gov

For information about infectious diseases go to the World Health Organization site at: www.who.int/topics/infectious_diseases

Drought and the Earth by Nikki Bundey (Zoe Books, 2000)

Fire in Their Eyes: Wildfires and the People Who Fight Them by Karen Magnuson Beil (Harcourt, 1999)

 Agronomist Researches ways to improve crops and the quality of seeds.

Epidemiologist Studies diseases and how they spread through populations.

Forest fire inspector Monitors the outbreaks of fires in national parks and forests.

Hydrologist Researches the quantity and distribution of underground and surface water.

Virologist Studies viruses and the diseases that they cause.

 Explore the health and medicine collection at the National Museum of American History, including penicillin mold from Alexander Fleming's original experiment and Jonas Salk's original polio vaccine. Smithsonian National Museum of American History National Mall Washington, D.C. 20560 Phone: (202) 633-1000 www.si.edu/visit/

See how the plague devastated London, England, during the 1300s at the Medieval London Gallery. The Museum of London London EC2Y 5HN, England Phone: 44 0 870 444 3852 www.museumoflondon.org.uk

Glossary

...ve volcano
...olcano that is erupting or is likely ...o so in the future.

...ressure
... weight of the atmosphere as it ...ses on the surface of the earth.

...biotic
...rug, such as penicillin, that is ...gned to treat bacterial infections.

... fine rock and mineral fragments
...ated during a volcanic eruption.

...enosphere
... semiliquid layer of molten rock ... lies beneath the lithosphere.

...osphere
... blanket of gases (mainly oxygen, ...rogen, and nitrogen) that forms ...envelope around the earth, ...ding it warm and protecting ...om the sun's radiation.

...teria
...roscopic organisms, some of which ... cause diseases.

...onic plague
...infectious and usually deadly ...demic disease transmitted by fleas.

...e
...inner part of the planet, consisting ... solid central core and a molten ...er core.

crater
A bowl-shaped hollow, often formed at the top of a volcano.

crust
The skin of rock that covers the surface of the earth.

cyclone
The name given to a hurricane in the Indian Ocean and western Pacific.

desert
An area, either hot or cold, where the annual rainfall is less than ten inches.

drought
Prolonged shortage of water, caused when less rain than normal falls.

A rescue dog searching for earthquake survivors

dyke
An embankment, often made of dirt, to prevent flooding.

epicenter
The point on the earth's surface that is directly above an earthquake's source.

epidemic
An outbreak of an infectious disease that affects a large number of people at the same time.

famine
A severe shortage of food, often caused by a drought.

fault
A fracture in the earth's crust where two plates move against each other.

flame retardant
A chemical or material that will not burn and is used by firefighters to control and slow down a blaze.

fossil fuels
Coal, oil, and natural gas formed millions of years ago by the decay and fossilization of organic matter.

glacier
A slow-moving river of ice made from compacted snow that flows down a valley under its own weight.

hypothermia
Dangerously low body temperature caused by exposure to cold and wind.

intestine
The long tube that forms the lower part of a person's digestive system.

irrigation
The supply of water to fields by means of pipes, streams, or channels dug into the ground.

lahar
Volcanic mudflow, often triggered by rapidly melting snow and ice, following a volcanic eruption.

lava
The word for magma after it has reached the earth's surface.

lithosphere
The surface, or outer layer, of the earth, that includes the crust and the upper part of the mantle.

magma
Molten rock formed under the earth's surface, just beneath the lithosphere.

magma chamber
An underground reservoir containing magma that feeds a volcano above.

magnitude
A measurement of the amount of energy released in an earthquake.

mantle
The thick layer of dense rock that makes up most of the planet and lies below the crust and above the core.

meteorologist
Scientist who studies the weather.

pandemic
An epidemic that affects large numbers of people across the world.

parasite
An organism that grows and feeds on another type of organism (such as an animal), but which does not do anything to benefit the host.

Lava flow from Kilauea, Hawaii

plate tectonics
The theory that the earth's surface is divided into a number of moving plates, causing continents to shift and new ocean crust to form, and triggering volcanoes and earthqua[...]

pneumonic plague
Infectious and deadly epidemic disease marked by inflammation and blockage of the lungs.

primary wave
A seismic wave that can travel through solid rock in the earth.

pyroclastic flow
Cloud made up of fragments of molten rock, ash, and volcani[...] gas, which is ejected from a volcano during an explosive eruption.

Cast of a human body found at Pompeii

...dar

...ystem used for detecting and
...ating distant objects, such as
...uds, that works by measuring the
...e it takes for radio waves to be
...lected back from the target.

...ervoir

...body of water collected in
...artificial or natural lake.

...g of Fire

...e region around the Pacific
...ean, where the Pacific plate
...eets other plates, and where
...st of the planet's volcanoes
...d earthquakes occur.

...pture

...break or tear in the earth's surface.

...ismic wave

...wave that runs through the earth,
...ually caused by an earthquake.

...ismograph

...instrument for detecting and
...cording the strength and
...rection of seismic waves.

...pticemic plague

...infectious and deadly epidemic
...sease in which microorganisms
...tack the blood system.

...ield volcano

...gently sloping volcano, formed
...om fast-flowing lava.

...orm surge

...rise in sea level that can cause
severe flooding in coastal areas.

tremor

A shaking or vibrating movement
in the earth's surface.

tropics

The warm regions to the north
and south of the equator.

troposphere

The lowest part of the atmosphere,
directly above the earth's surface.

tsunamis

Waves, or series of waves, generated
by a massive displacement of water,
caused by earthquakes or explosive
volcanic eruptions on the coast.

turbulence

Air that has become very agitated.

updraft

A movement of air away from the
ground, typically found inside
thunderstorms and tornadoes.

vaccination

A medicine, often given by injection,
that protects against a disease.

vent

An opening inside the earth's crust
that allows volcanic gases and
molten rock to escape.

virus

A tiny chemical package that invades
living cells and causes diseases.

An overpass
destroyed by
an earthquake
in Kobe, Japan

water vapor

Water in the form of gas.

waterspout

A spinning column of wind that
sucks water up from lakes and seas.

weather balloon

A balloon used to carry
meteorological instruments.

Index

Acknowledgments

The publisher would like to thank the following for permission to reproduce their material. Every care has been taken to trace copyright holders. However, if there have been unintentional omissions or failure to trace copyright holders, we apologize and will, if informed, endeavor to make corrections in any future edition.

Key: *b* = bottom, *c* = center, *l* = left, *r* = right, *t* = top

Cover *left* Getty/Paula Bronstein; Cover *center* Corbis/Raymond Gehman; Cover *center background* Corbis/Stephen Dol; Cover *right* Corbis/Reuters; Cover *bottom* Getty Stone; page 1 Empics/AP; 2*l* Corbis/ Reuters; 2–3 Getty/NGS; 4–5 Corbis/Reuters; 7 Corbis/Charles O'Rear; 8*tl* Corbis/Reuters; 8–9 Corbis/Reuters; 9*tr* Science Photo Library (SPL); 10*tl* SPL/David Parker; 10*b* Getty/Hulton; 11*b* Corbis/Grant Smith; 11*tr* Getty/Koichi Kamoshida; 12*bl* Getty/Photonica; 13*tl* Getty/Time Life Pictures; 13*bl* Getty/AFP/Bay Ismoyo; 14*tr* Science & Society Picture Library; 14*tl* Getty/AFP; 14*b* Getty/Spencer Platt; 15*b* Corbis/Punit Paranjpe/ Reuters; 15*tr* Getty/AFP/Sena Vidanagama; 16*tl* Science & Society Picture Library; 16*bl* Corbis/Reuters; 17*bl* Popperfoto/Reuters; 17*tr* SPL/British Antarctic Survey; 19 Getty/NGS; 20*tl* SPL/Mark Garlick; 20*bl* SPL/Gary Hincks; 20–21 Getty; 21*br* SPL/Christian Darkin; 21*tr* Corbis/Pierre Vauthey; 22*bl* Art Archive; 22*br*(b) SPL/Stephen & Donna O' Meara; 22*br*(c) SPL/G Brad Lewis; 22*br*(t) SPL/G Brad Lewis; 23*br* Planet Earth; 23*t* Getty/Imagebank; 24*tl*(t) Corbis; 24*tl*(b) Corbis; 24*bl* Corbis/Roger Ressmeyer; 24*cr* Frank Spooner Pictures/NASA/Liaison/B Ingalls; 25 Corbis; 26*tl* Getty Hulton; 26*bl* SPL/Robert M. Carey/NOAA; 27*br* Panos Pictures; 28*bl* SPL/NASA; 28*tr* Corbis/Yann Arthus–Bertrand; 28–29 Getty NGS; 30 Art Archive; 31 Getty/NGS; 32*cl* SPL/R. B. Huser/NASA; 32–33 SPL/Jim Reed; 32*tr* SPL/John Beatty; 33*b* SPL/Jim Reed; 33*tr* Sygma/ Bleibtreu/John Hillelson Agency; 34*bl* SPL/NOAA; 34–35 Getty/Photonica; 35*br* Corbis/Roger Bell; 36–37 Photolibrary.com; 37*bl* Photolibrary.com; 37*tr* Getty/AFP/Farjana Godhuly; 38*tl* Corbis/Reuters; 38*b* Corbis Historical Picture Archive; 39*tl* Corbis/Reuters; 39*cr* Getty/Hulton; 39*b* Corbis/Sygma; 40*tr* Empics; 40–41 Empics; 41*tl* SPL/NASA; 41*tr* Corbis Bettmann; 42*tl* Corbis Reuters; 42*bl* Rex Features; 42–43*t* SPL/W. Bacon; 42–43*b* Zefa; 43*bl* Corbis/David Lees; 44*cl* SPL/Peter Menzel; 44–45*b* Getty/NGS; 45*br* Rex Features; 46*tl* Corbis/Reuters; 47*t* Corbis/China Photo/Reuters; 48*bl* NOAA; 48–49 Still Pictures/Hartmut Schwarzbach; 50*tr* Getty/David Hume–Kennerly; 50*cl* Getty/Stone; 50–51 Getty/Stone; 51*b* Getty/David McNew; 51*t* Getty/David McNew; 52*tl* SPL/Russell Kightley; 52*cl* SPL/Eye of Science; 52–53 Corbis/Timothy Fadek; 53*br* Corbis/Dadang Tri/Reuters; 53*tr* SPL/Biomedical Imaging Unit, Southampton General Hospital; 54*tl* SPL/John Burbidge; 54*bl* Frank Lane Picture Agency/Foto Natura; 54–55*c* Corbis/Nicole Duplaix; 55*bl* Mary Evans Picture Library; 55*br* SPL; 55*tr* SPL/U.S. Library of Medicine; 56*b* Corbis/Caroline Penn; 56–57 Getty/NGS; 57*br* SPL/S. Nagendra; 57*tr* SPL/Laurent/Bsip; 58*cl* Getty/Stone; 59*b* Corbis/Owen Franken; 60*tr* Getty/Taxi; 60*bl* Corbis/Roger Ressmeyer; 61*tr* Corbis/Reuters; 64 Corbis/Reuters

The publisher would like to thank the following illustrators: Sebastien Quigley (Linden Artists) (12–13, 32–33, 34–35, 42–43, 50–51); Peter Clayman (36–37)

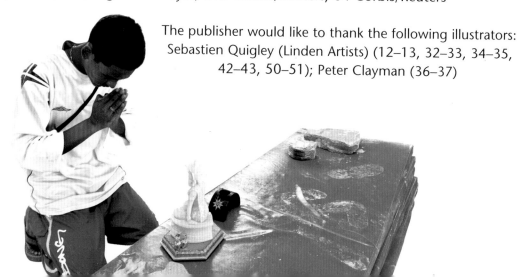